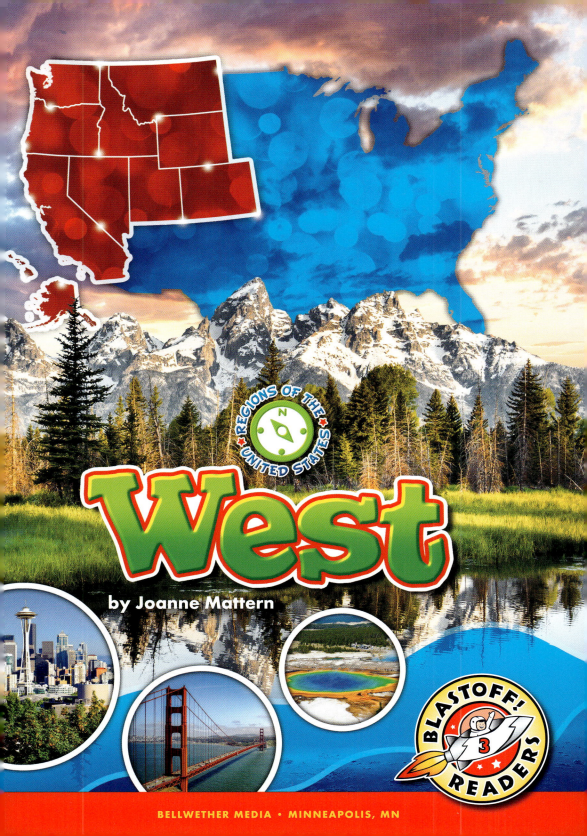

West

by Joanne Mattern

Blastoff! Readers are carefully developed by literacy experts to build reading stamina and move students toward fluency by combining standards-based content with developmentally appropriate text.

LEVELS

Level 1 provides the most support through repetition of high-frequency words, light text, predictable sentence patterns, and strong visual support.

Level 2 offers early readers a bit more challenge through varied sentences, increased text load, and text-supportive special features.

Level 3 advances early-fluent readers toward fluency through increased text load, less reliance on photos, advancing concepts, longer sentences, and more complex special features.

★ **Blastoff! Universe**

Reading Level

Grade K

Grades 1–3

Grade 4

This edition first published in 2025 by Bellwether Media, Inc.

No part of this publication may be reproduced in whole or in part without written permission of the publisher. For information regarding permission, write to Bellwether Media, Inc., Attention: Permissions Department, 6012 Blue Circle Drive, Minnetonka, MN 55343.

Library of Congress Cataloging-in-Publication Data

Names: Mattern, Joanne, 1963- author.
Title: West / by Joanne Mattern.
Description: Minneapolis, MN : Bellwether Media, Inc., 2025. | Series: Blastoff! Readers : regions of the United States | Includes bibliographical references and index. | Audience: Ages 5-8 | Audience: Grades 2-3 | Summary: "Simple text and full-color photography introduce beginning readers to the West. Developed by literacy experts for students in kindergarten through third grade"-- Provided by publisher.
Identifiers: LCCN 2024039175 (print) | LCCN 2024039176 (ebook) | ISBN 9798893042511 (library binding) | ISBN 9798893043488 (ebook)
Subjects: LCSH: West (U.S.)--Juvenile literature.
Classification: LCC F591 .M327 2025 (print) | LCC F591 (ebook) | DDC 978--dc23/eng/20240910
LC record available at https://lccn.loc.gov/2024039175
LC ebook record available at https://lccn.loc.gov/2024039176

Text copyright © 2025 by Bellwether Media, Inc. BLASTOFF! READERS and associated logos are trademarks and/or registered trademarks of Bellwether Media, Inc.

Editor: Kieran Downs   Designer: Brittany McIntosh

Printed in the United States of America, North Mankato, MN.

Table of Contents

Welcome to the West! 4
The Land, Weather, and Wildlife 6
Natural Resources and Industry 12
People of the West 14
West Fast Facts 20
Glossary 22
To Learn More 23
Index 24

Welcome to the West!

The West is a region of the United States. The region includes 11 states.

The West is filled with beautiful places. The region also has many important **industries**.

States in the West

The Land, Weather, and Wildlife

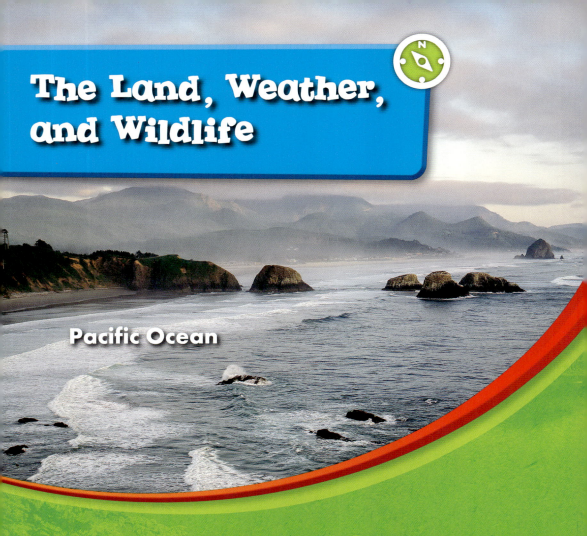

Pacific Ocean

The West has different kinds of land. Some areas lie along the coast of the Pacific Ocean. **Temperate rainforests** grow in northern coastal areas.

Other areas feature deserts or mountains. **Plains** make up the eastern part of the region.

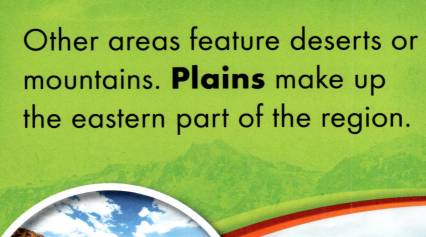
desert

plains

Many parts of the West have an **arid** climate. Some places on the coast are cool and wet.

Alaska and areas in the mountains get a lot of snow. The islands of Hawaii are hot all year long.

Yellowstone National Park

Location: Montana, Idaho, Wyoming

Famous For: The world's first national park

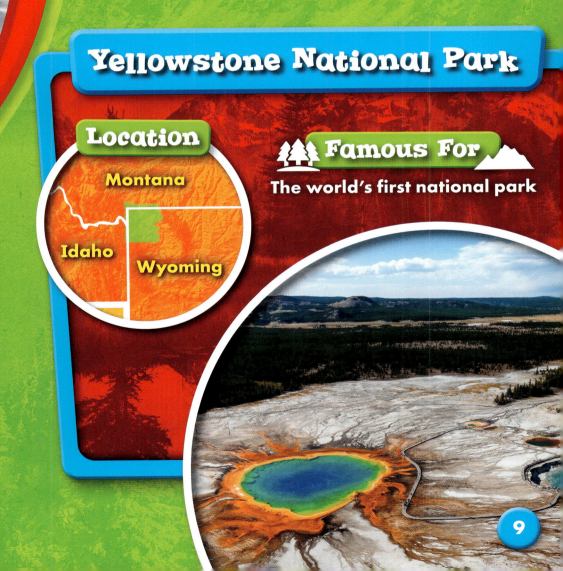

Many large animals live in the West. Bison live on the plains. Elk and bears live in the mountains.

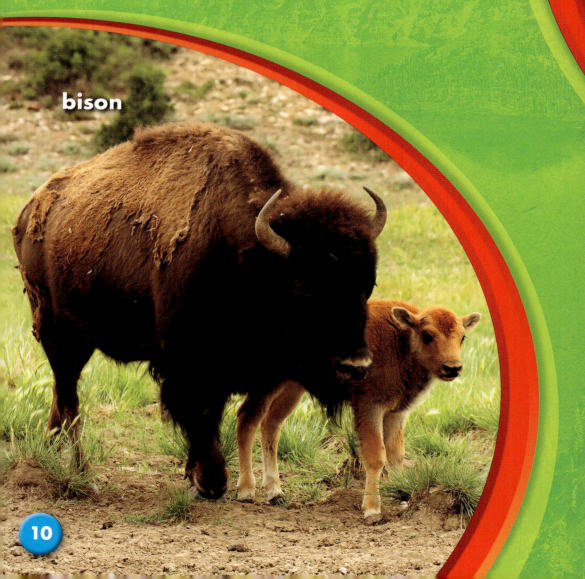

bison

rattlesnake

salmon

Reptiles live in Western deserts. They include lizards and rattlesnakes. Salmon swim in rivers. Frogs live in streams and ponds.

Natural Resources and Industry

pineapple field

Farmers in California and Hawaii grow many fruits. These include oranges, lemons, grapes, and pineapples. **Ranchers** raise many animals.

Many people in the West work in the **technology** industry. Others cut **timber** in forests.

Resource to Industry
Lumber Production

large forests

trees for lumber

People of the West

Los Angeles, California

Native Americans were the first people to live in the West. Many people today have Native American **ancestors**. Others have European, Asian, or Hispanic ancestors.

Most people live in **urban** areas. Los Angeles, California, is the largest city in the region.

People in the West eat many tasty foods. Mexican foods are popular in California. Idaho is known for its potatoes. Huckleberries grow in Montana.

Mexican food

Many people catch salmon in the rivers of the West. These fish are good to eat!

People in the West enjoy outdoor activities. They like to hike, fish, and camp. They ski in the mountains.

Millions of people visit **national parks** each year. There is always something to do in the West!

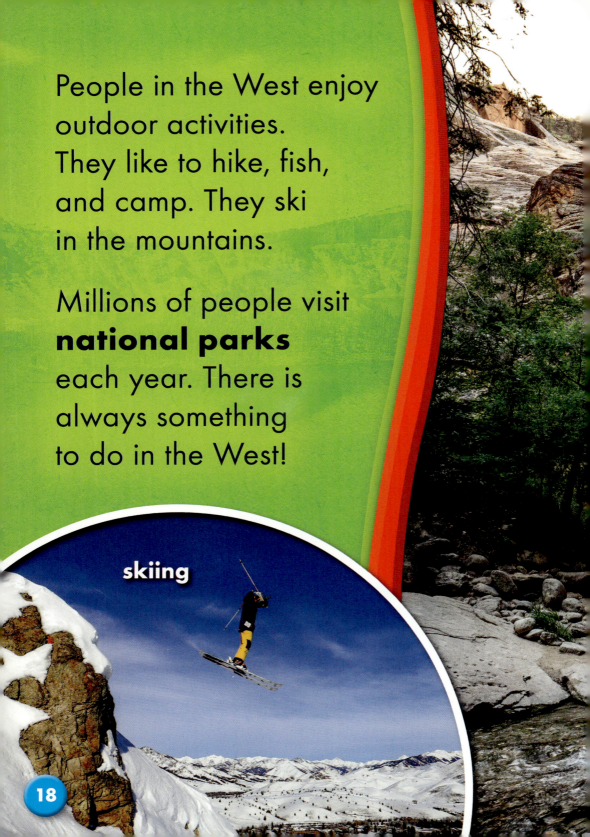

skiing

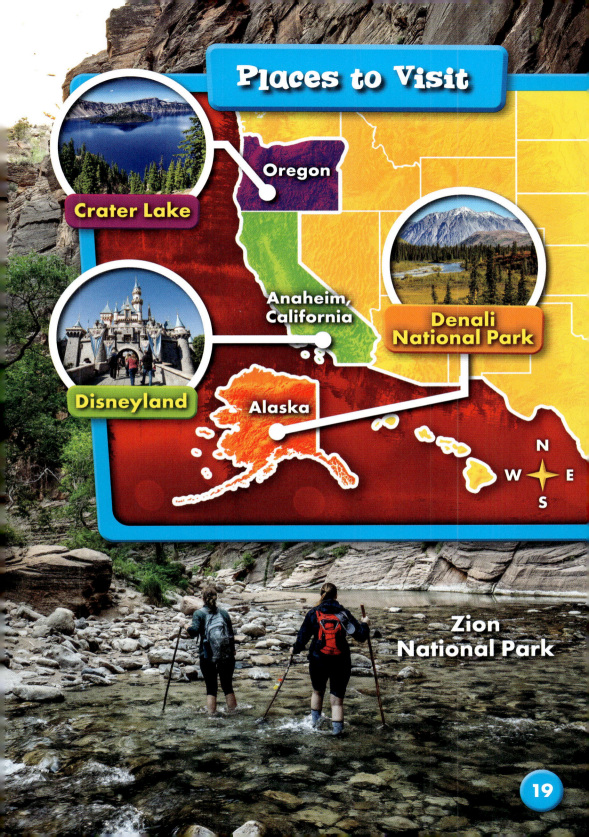

West Fast Facts

3 Largest Cities (2020)

1. Los Angeles, California
Population: around 3.9 million

2. San Diego, California
Population: around 1.4 million

3. San Jose, California
Population: around 1 million

State Populations (2020)

- Alaska: 733,391
- Washington: 7.7 million
- Idaho: 1.8 million
- Montana: 1.1 million
- Oregon: 4.2 million
- Colorado: 5.8 million
- Hawaii: 1.5 million
- Nevada: 3.1 million
- Wyoming: 576,851
- California: 39.5 million
- Utah: 3.3 million

Major Sports Teams

Los Angeles Dodgers
(MLB)

Las Vegas Raiders
(NFL)

Denver Nuggets
(NBA)

Famous Face

Name: Dwayne "The Rock" Johnson
Hometown: Hayward, California
Famous for: Popular actor and wrestler

Smallest State

Hawaii
10,932 square miles
(28,314 square kilometers)

Largest State

Alaska
665,384 square miles
(1,723,337 square kilometers)

Glossary

ancestors—relatives who lived long ago

arid—very dry, with little rainfall

industries—groups of businesses that provide certain products or services

national parks—areas of land that a country sets aside for natural or historic reasons

plains—areas of flat land with few trees

ranchers—people who work on large farms that raise horses, beef cattle, or sheep

reptiles—cold-blooded animals that have backbones and lay eggs

technology—using knowledge to invent new devices or tools

temperate rainforests—thick, green forests that have mild temperatures and receive a lot of rain

timber—wood that is used for building

urban—related to cities or city life

To Learn More

AT THE LIBRARY

Harrison, Audrey. *Alaska*. Minneapolis, Minn.: Abdo Publishing, 2023.

Khor, Shing Yin. *What Made California the Golden State?: Life During the Gold Rush*. New York, N.Y.: Penguin Workshop, 2024.

Spanier, Kristine. *Explore the West*. Minneapolis, Minn.: Jump!, 2023.

ON THE WEB

FACTSURFER

Factsurfer.com gives you a safe, fun way to find more information.

1. Go to www.factsurfer.com.

2. Enter "West" into the search box and click 🔍.

3. Select your book cover to see a list of related content.

Index

ancestors, 14
animals, 10, 11, 12, 17
climate, 8, 9
farmers, 12
fast facts, 20–21
foods, 16, 17
industries, 5, 13
land, 6, 7, 9, 10, 11, 13, 17, 18
Los Angeles, California, 14, 15
map, 5
national parks, 18
outdoor activities, 18
Pacific Ocean, 6
people, 13, 14, 15, 16, 17, 18
places to visit, 19
ranchers, 12
resource to industry, 13
states, 4, 5, 9, 12, 15, 16
technology, 13
Yellowstone National Park, 9

The images in this book are reproduced through the courtesy of: Pat Tr, front cover (main); Agnieszka Gaul, front cover (bottom left); EliteCustomAdventures.com, front cover (bottom center); Lorcel, front cover (bottom right); photomaster, p. 3; Peter Kunasz, p. 4; julius fekete, p. 6; Beketoff, p. 7 (top); Takeshi Bennet, p. 7 (bottom); Troutnut, p. 8 (top); Art Wager, p. 8 (bottom); Pandora Pictures, p. 9; MelaniWright, p. 10; Audrey Snider-Bell, p. 11 (top); The Old Major, p. 11 (bottom); ShishkaBob, p. 12; Jon Bilous, p. 13 (left); TFoxFoto, p. 13 (right); Harun Ozmen, p. 14; Danita Delimont, p. 15; Brannon_Naito, p. 16; Jacek Chabraszewski, p. 17 (top); Wollertz, p. 17 (bottom); CSNafzger, p. 18; Ryan Kelehar, pp. 18-19; ORCHID LADY, p. 19 (Crater Lake); Michael DeFreitas North America/ Alamy, p. 19 (Disneyland); Uwe Bergwitz, p. 19 (Denali National Park); Emeric's Timelapse, p. 20 (Los Angeles); ByDroneVideos, p. 20 (San Diego); Uladzik Kryhin, p. 20 (San Jose); Los Angeles Dodgers/ Wikipedia, p. 21 (Dodgers logo); Las Vegas Raiders/ Wikipedia, p. 21 (Raiders logo); Denver Nuggets/ Wikipedia, p. 21 (Nuggets logo); Jaguar PS, p. 21 (Dwayne Johnson); Tiger Images, p. 23.